SELLING
LIFE INSURANCE:
Rising to a Higher Income

Jim Van Houten

CLU, MSFS, ChFC, MSM

THIS BOOK IS DEDICATED TO OUR SONS:

JAMESON, JERED, JEFFREY, AND JAKOB.

Table of Contents

Introduction 6

1 Building a Prospecting System 9

How do you develop these sources? 15

Your Personal Prospecting System 27

2 The Case for Cash Value Life Insurance 32

3 Where Cash Value Life Insurance is Needed 36

Estate Planning 36

Buy Sell Life Insurance 41

Key Person Benefit Plans 44

Charitable Planned Giving 50

Retirement Maximization 52

Asset Protection 54

In Summary 56

4 Well Organized Activity 57

A Final Note 61

VAN HOUTENISMS: Words of Wisdom from Jim 63

About the Author 66

Note: For ease of communication, I have used the male gender where it could equally be male or female.

Introduction

Selling life insurance can be a rewarding and profitable career. It is rewarding to be able to provide financial stability for the family that just lost a loved one. When a death occurs, life insurance comes in to rescue families from financial hardships.

As an agent selling life insurance, you perform a very valuable service. You deserve to be well paid for that service. Unfortunately, we are not often appreciated until it is time to deliver a check.

Sometimes you invent fancy titles for your occupation: family security specialist, financial advisor, insurance consultant. Sometimes you find yourself alone in a crowd when you say that you sell life insurance.

Be proud of what you do. Others go to a funeral and express their sympathy. You go with the knowledge that you will be bringing the family a check that will keep the family financially secure, that will pay off all debts and the mortgage, that will educate the children.

You must have conviction in what you do. To be really successful in the life insurance business, you must own a substantial amount of life insurance to sell a substantial amount of life insurance. When you personally pay a lot in premiums, you will be stronger in asking someone else to pay a lot in premiums. People sense it when you really believe in what you are proposing.

You have to be your own positive reinforcement of the good that you do. It can be a hard business especially on your attitude because of all the rejection you receive. Since it is so hard, it pays well.

The purpose of this book is to provide you

with additional tools to help you sell larger quantities of life insurance to higher quality clients. This involves creative prospecting, focusing on situations where permanent life insurance is needed and well-organized activity management.

I have helped thousands of agents, both new and experienced, increase their sales and incomes through the ideas in this book. My goal is to help you enjoy a higher income from your life insurance sales.

First, you need to have a prospecting system that generates quality prospects for you on a regular and consistent basis.

1

Building a Prospecting System

Maybe you recall that at a sales seminar you heard someone mention having a prospecting system. That sounded like a good idea. So, you ask yourself, how do you get one of those systems?

You ask yourself: maybe I need to set up a website so people will google it and send in requests for life insurance. Or maybe you can get a robot-dialer to send texts to random numbers. Or buy a Facebook ad. Or buy a list of "qualified names" from some company. No, none of these makes sense.

A prospecting system is a coordinated program that generates qualified prospects for you on a regular and consistent basis with minimal effort from you. Qualified prospects are those people that you believe meet your criteria of someone that you would like to have as a client.

When you first started selling life insurance, a qualified prospect was anyone that could pass the physical and pay the premium. To grow your business, you will want to become more selective as to what is a qualified prospect for you. You will want to raise your criteria.

Some people are one-time buyers and not really clients. Some buyers will not grow much in income or make future purchases. With these people, you will want to provide service as needed but not include them in the list of clients that you meet with regularly.

A client has trust and confidence in you. It is the development of an advisory relationship that you seek. You will then no longer be considered by the clients as a sales person selling them life insurance. You are their adviser helping them to buy life insurance. **You talk differently to a client than you do to a prospect.**

What will be your new criteria for qualified prospects? Your new criteria will probably include a minimum annual income. It may include a minimum net worth. Perhaps it will include consideration of occupation or business ownership. Maybe you will consider family situation. You may also want to include potential for growth and ability to refer you to others in similar circumstances. You need to decide first what your criteria will be.

Now that you have your new criteria for qualified prospects, let's look at some excellent sources of qualified prospects:

- Your **existing clients** that meet your new criteria. Statistics show that clients will buy at least 6 times in their lifetimes and the last purchase will be the largest one.

- **Referrals from clients** – referrals from people who already do business with you are strong referrals since your clients will strongly endorse you and know what kind of person you want.

- **Family and close friends** – family and close friends already know you. They also know that you have survived the difficult beginning years of this career (most agents do not make it past three years in the business). They may not always buy what you recommend but they will buy from you if you ask. I am always surprised when an agent tells me that he never asked his family or close friends.

- **Orphans** of an insurance company that you do business with – every insurance company has policyholders who no longer have an active agent relationship with someone associated with the insurance company. You will want to promise the insurance company that you will protect the orphans' coverage with that insurance company.

- **Referrals from centers of influence** such as attorneys, CPAs, financial advisors, property and casualty insurance agents, luxury car sales persons. Centers of influence usually have a professional relationship with the qualified prospects. The referral respects the center's advice and recommendations.

- **Referrals from non-clients** – sometimes you develop a strong relationship with someone who, for reasons beyond your control, does not buy from you. This person may want to make up for not buying from you by sending you quality people who will.

- **Social** – people like to do business with people they know. There are many opportunities to meet people socially through your children's activities, your church, country club, service club, charity activities, etc.

- **Targeting** – this is finding a way get an introduction to someone that you would like to meet and develop into a client.

How do you develop these sources?

With regard to **existing clients** that meet your new criteria, you should conduct annual reviews. The best date for the review is the month before their insurance age changes. If additional life insurance is needed, buying it before a rate increase is a strong motivator. In addition, you should have a questionnaire emailed to them two months before the age change. You are looking for any changes that might indicate a need for additional coverage.

When doing a review, you will want to plant the seeds of future expansion of the client's life insurance program. Then you are ready to ask your clients for referrals.

Before you **ask a client for referrals**, remind him that you are not asking who does he know that wants to buy life insurance today. That implies that the client knows the financial affairs of their friends, which they probably do not. Rather, you are asking about people who have had life changes recently. I used to say that I do not know who wants to buy life insurance today and I am in the business.

Use a *Who Do You Know* list. It will stimulate names. Ask each question and then <u>wait</u> for a response before going to the next question. Give them time to think of names.

Here are some of the questions that I would ask. You may want to add some of your own.

Who do you know that:

- Has a vacation home?
- Owns a luxury car?
- Purchased a new home?
- Is a CEO or CFO of a successful business?
- Bought or sold a business?
- Was complaining about income taxes?
- Expanded his family?
- _____

Most people have over one hundred names stored in their cell phone contact list. That means that the potential is there for over one hundred referrals. Ask your client to take out his cell phone and bring up the contact list. Then start with A and end with Z. You will get a lot of names. Get the names first and then go back to get more details on each name.

When you first get referrals, your referrer will probably give you three or more of his B-list referrals and then wait to see how you do. He will keep in reserve the A-list referrals because he does not want to be embarrassed by you to his A-list friends. Knowing that, it is very important that you report back to the referrer what happened with each referral that he gave you. Then ask him for more referrals. Now you will usually get the A-list referrals. Always report back to clients what happened with the referrals.

Anyone in the business will tell you that it is

challenging to do business with **family and close friends**. You would think that if anyone should trust you with their life insurance, it would be family and close friends. They have known you for a long time and know your values. However, they also know how long you have been in the business and they may carry memories of past challenges you have had.

You have a serious responsibility to take care of your family and close friends. Imagine going to the funeral for a family member or close friend and the widowed spouse says to you: "How much life insurance did John (the deceased) have with you?" You then answer: "None. I never asked him to buy any".

Even if your family member or close friend does not buy from you initially, you need to ask for the opportunity to do a summary of his existing coverage. Do not give up. Keep asking over the years. You can get a lot of No but need only one Yes. You have a moral obligation to take care of those who love and care for you. Do not let your ego get in the way of your responsibility.

When you find **orphans**, adopt them. There are hundreds of life insurance companies. Most of the companies do not have career agents. Even the big insurance companies have frequent turnover of career agents. Policyholders often find themselves without a relationship with an agent. They do not have someone to provide guidance and service.

When you find someone who owns a life insurance policy and does not have a current agent, contact the life insurance company and seek a servicing relationship with that life insurance company. Sell the insurance company on your experience, your professionalism and your ethics to serve their policyholders as the insurance company would want their policyholders to be serviced. Ask the insurance company to send you information on any other policyholders in your area. Tell them that you promise to meet with each of the policyholders they send to you. Tell them that you will review their beneficiary arrangements and service the policies in the future. Let them know that you will protect the policy from being replaced by other agents.

This worked well for me over the years. The orphan will probably be receptive to your approach since you are representing the company that the orphan is currently paying money to. This reduces the normal resistance that prospects have to meeting with you.

One orphan I picked up this way turned out to be the CEO of a very large company. He had not met with a life insurance agent in many years. This resulted in several substantial sales and referrals.

Once you get several companies sending you orphans, you will be surprised how many you get and that they keep sending you more. Some of the orphans I got were business owners and other professionals. It is important to report back to the life insurance company what happened with your meeting with the orphans. I also used other agents in my office to follow up with the orphans that did not fit my criteria of a qualified prospect.

Referrals from centers of influence are very beneficial. A center of influence is someone that has influence over the referral. This person may be an attorney, a CPA, a financial advisor, property and casualty insurance agent, or a luxury car salesperson. It may be a successful business person. You may find this person on a charitable board. You may find this person through your children's activities.

Finding the right person who is willing to refer people to you is a big part of the challenge. You will need to educate the person about you, the type of work that you do, the process you follow when given a name, and your level of professionalism. Initially, you will need to ask for referrals in person and report back in person. It is like a training process. Eventually the centers will send qualified prospects to you without you having to ask.

There is an old adage that out of sight is out of mind. With centers of influence this is especially true. You will want to schedule regular quarterly meetings with them and have monthly email reminders go to them. Once you get a good center of influence developed, the flow of qualified prospects will surprise you.

Look for articles, quotes, sales ideas that you can send to centers. You never know what may trigger a referral in their minds. Be sure that they have your cell phone number so they may call or text you anytime with a referral.

A very beneficial source of potential centers of influence is the members of an estate planning council. An estate planning council is made up of attorneys, CPAs, trust officers, and life insurance professionals. Through these meetings and study groups within the council, you will get to know these other professionals very well. You may find that some of them can be developed into centers for you. Be sure to refer people back to your centers as often as you are able. They understand the value of referrals.

Referrals from non-clients. Am I serious? Yes! Sometimes, you develop a terrific relationship with a prospect but in the end, they do not buy from you. Most agents will take their file and shred it.

Why waste a good relationship? Seek to develop them into a referral source. Most people appreciate when you spend time with them, giving them worthwhile advice and service. They feel obligated to you. You should give them a chance to pay you for your time with quality referrals.

Some agents have found that they can get good quality referrals from non-clients. Frequently the referrer becomes a client.

Social prospecting scares most agents. These agents are so afraid of developing a reputation of soliciting all of their friends that they do not ever ask social contacts. To overcome this reluctance, it takes both a change in mental attitude and a plan for approaching them.

You must sincerely believe that you do bring great value to your clients. Even if you get rejected, you will need to not take it personally. You will need to act as professionally as possible. I have found it to be effective to ask the prospect to have lunch or a drink together.

At that meeting, you will want to ask them about their business (what do they do, how did they get into it, how is the business doing, what are the big issues affecting the business, etc.). This may take 20 minutes. Be a good listener and keep them talking. Eventually they will ask you about your business. Start by explaining what makes you different (your education, your experience,

RISING TO A HIGHER INCOME

your ethics). Next, explain what you do to help clients (correct beneficiaries, planning tools, make life insurance more cost effective, etc.). Offer them a free review of their existing coverages.

I want to share a story to illustrate this. I coached Little League for 18 years. One day I asked the father of one of my players to go to lunch. We had spoken often before and after games about his son. I found out that he was a divorced doctor with four children and was engaged to be married. I asked for the opportunity to review his life insurance and disability insurance coverages and do a summary for him. He agreed but assured me that he was entirely satisfied with his existing agent. My review confirmed that the beneficiary of all his life insurance was still his ex-wife. He was shocked! He had asked his existing agent four years before to change the beneficiary to his fiancé. I then produced forms to change the beneficiary on his policies right then. He signed the forms and

25

declared me his new agent. He became a very good client and referral source.

Targeting begins with the identifying of a person that you would like to approach. This may be a person you heard about on social media or the news. It may be someone that you heard of through a charitable activity or someone that is well known in the business world. You will then start asking your clients, centers of influence and friends if they know this person. You will keep asking people until you find a connection. Then you will approach this person as you would a referral.

It took me two years to find a connection to the CEO of a Fortune 100 company. It took me two months to finally get on his calendar. Once we met, I was surprised to find that he was so well insulated by assistants that he had not met with a life insurance adviser in many years. Often the harder it is to get an appointment with someone, the more likely it is that the person does not have a current life insurance adviser. He became a wonderful client and referral source.

A key point to remember is that wealthy people are like elephants. They run in herds. Once you get a few wealthy clients, you will be introduced to their wealthy friends. You will be invited to social events with them. If you treat them well, you will be referred to their friends.

Your Personal Prospecting System

Now to developing your personal prospecting system. You will want the system to be automatic and efficient. As much as possible computerize your process.

The first step is to put on your calendar all the **annual reviews with existing clients** listing them in the month before their insurance age change. This should give you a number of meetings each month that could generate additional sales and give you an opportunity to ask for referrals. Your goals are to look for additional life insurance needs and to use the Who Do You Know questions to generate at least 3 high quality referrals. With your better clients, you will want to go through their cell phone contact list looking for referrals.

Next, **follow up on client referrals** as soon as possible. Try to do so within a week or two. You will be more excited about referrals if you follow up right away. Delay causes you to lose interest and that can make the referrals stale. You may want to use a letter or email of introduction or make a phone call to set up an appointment. If you get a negative response from the prospect, I suggest that you say: "Things have a way of changing, may I call you back in 90 days?" Then put the referral on your calendar for a call back in 90 days.

Make a point of **following up with family and close friends**, who are not already clients, within the first two months of starting your **personal prospecting system**. Once and for all time, ask them to do business with you. If they refuse your request, document their answer and then forget them as prospects.

Starting in the third month of **your personal prospecting system**, contact your first insurance company to ask about **orphans**. Every three months thereafter, contact another insurance company. It will take time and a few emails to finally convince these companies to trust you with their policyholders. As you contact the orphans, you can decide which ones fit your criteria as a qualified prospect. The rest of the orphans you can give to an associate.

Once you have the relationships established with these life insurance companies, orphans will continue to come to you for years as policyholders move into your area.

An important part of **your prospecting system** is the development of **centers of**

influence. You must first identify those people that you know that could be good centers. Meet with them to ask their help. Keep your eyes open for additional potential centers. Getting a center of influence is like making a sale so prepare well for the time you meet with them. Then put the centers on your calendar to meet with them quarterly. Set them up on your email list so they will receive ideas and articles from you. Make sure to report back to the centers about the referrals they provide.

Referrals from non-clients will occur as sales situations arise. It requires an attitude change on your part. Instead of lingering in disappointment, turn it into anticipation of getting more qualified prospects.

Social prospecting occurs as you get involved either in your children's activities, charitable work or both. Take a leadership role. Let others see that you have a passion for what you are doing. Be active.

Target marketing was fun for me. I would hear of someone that I would like as a client. Then I would talk to clients, friends and family to find someone who could refer me to him. It may take months but I would keep looking. This is exactly how I got several clients who are worth more than $50 million.

Here is an important fact of about prospecting:

Unseen and Untold is Unsold!

Hopefully, by now, you have developed your prospecting system and incorporated the prospecting ideas outlined above. Remember **STP! See the People!** Now we can focus on situations where permanent life insurance is needed.

2

The Case for Cash Value Life Insurance

If you are going to earn a higher income in this business, you can either sell a lot of term insurance or sell more cash value life insurance. By cash value life insurance, I mean whole life or universal life.

These policies build up cash values. They have a minimum guaranteed interest rate of earnings. They may pay an excess interest above the guaranteed rate or pay dividends. Either way, the interest earnings on permanent life insurance are competitive with bank savings accounts, certificates of deposit and bonds.

These policies have a level premium. Coverage continues for life (guaranteed in whole life) or until the policy runs out of money (for universal life).

With the addition of the Waiver of Premium rider, you have a self-completing policy if the insured becomes totally disabled. The cash values would continue to grow without the owner paying any more premiums.

Cash value life insurance is sometimes criticized by those advocating "buy term and invest the difference". The advocates of this philosophy always compare the returns of the cash value policies to stock mutual funds, gold, real estate, or silver.

The critics use whatever investment they are currently selling. They always use partial past performance to predict that the future will always produce the same result. My point is that they are comparing apples and oranges.

Cash value life insurance contains guarantees (guaranteed cash values and guaranteed minimum interest rate) and the investments have no guarantees. Investments have the risk of losing the principal. Cash value life insurance has a guarantee of principal. Cash value life insurance should be compared to bank savings or bonds. That result would show that cash value life insurance can outperform bank savings or bonds. Cash value life insurance provides stable and consistent growth in cash values

Cash value life insurance accumulates cash values on a tax deferred basis. The interest and dividend earnings are not taxed until the policy is surrendered. You can borrow out most of the cash values without incurring taxes.

Having lifetime level premiums is an advantage not to be discounted. Term life insurance buyers find out the hard way that renewing term life insurance in your 60s or

70s is very expensive. I had a client recently who was age 65 and no change in medical history. His old 15 Year term premium for $2 million of coverage was $800 a month. The new premium was over $40,000 a year. This was with the same underwriting classification. As you get older, premiums go up exponentially.

Statistics have proven that only 2% of term life insurance ever becomes a claim. It is also true that 100% of cash value life insurance over three years old provides a benefit (either death benefit or cash values).

With term life insurance, if you miss a premium then the policy lapses. With cash value life insurance, if you miss a premium then the insurance company uses existing cash values to keep the policy going.

Let's look at situations where cash value life insurance is needed and appropriate.

3

Where Cash Value Life Insurance is Needed

Estate Planning

No matter the size of the estate, everyone is going to die. When that happens, cash is needed to pay final medical expenses, funeral service fees, burial plot and coffin or cremation, and any remaining debts. Life insurance is ideal because it pays cash for these expenses relieving families from depleting savings, borrowing or selling investments to pay these expenses.

In larger estates, there are State and Federal Estate Taxes which are also called death taxes. The tax is on the transfer of assets to people other than a spouse. In 2020, the individual's estate had to be over $11.58 million (exemption amount) before this was a concern. The exemption amount is adjusted each year for inflation. The top estate tax bracket is 40%. For married couples, there is no tax on the transfer of assets from a deceased spouse to the surviving spouse. Upon the death of the surviving spouse, the estate tax is charged.

For example, consider a couple with a $50 million estate. When the first spouse dies, all the assets pass to the surviving spouse tax free. When the surviving spouse dies, there will be a tax on the transfer of the assets to their heirs.

First, the exemption amount is deducted from the assets to determine the taxable estate ($50 million estate minus $11.58 million exemption amount= $38.42 million taxable estate). Then tax rate of 40% is applied to the taxable estate to determine the taxes due ($38.42 million times 40% = $15.368 million tax due).

If the couple utilizes a properly designed trust, then when the first spouse dies, the deceased's exemption amount ($11.58 million) is set aside tax free. When the surviving spouse dies, the second exemption amount is subtracted from the remaining estate ($38.42 million minus $11.58 million= $26.84 million). Using the same 40% tax rate, the tax due would be $10.736 million.

The tax is payable in cash and must be paid within 9 months of death. The forced sale of assets to pay the taxes can result in substantial loss of values to the family. There are estate vultures out there who will offer heirs 50% of value for estate assets because they know that heirs have to raise a lot of cash in less than 9 months. Life insurance can provide the cash necessary to pay estate taxes without causing the heirs to quickly sell assets.

There is a unique type of life insurance developed just for estate planning. It is called Survivorship Life. It insures two people but does not pay off until the second person dies. In the case of an insured married couple, the life insurance does not pay off when the first spouse dies. It will pay off when the surviving spouse dies, which is when the estate tax is incurred.

The policy must be a cash value life insurance policy because the policy must be kept in force for life. Once you get a policy placed to cover estate taxes, then you will want to periodically review with the clients the size of their estates to see if an increase in coverage is needed.

I have found it advantageous to quote the premium for the life insurance as a percentage of the life insurance benefit. For example, if the premium is $100,000 on a $5 million policy, I would quote the premium as 2% of the life insurance benefit. At that rate, it would take 50 years to pay in premium equal to what will be paid off at death. It sounds a lot better to say that the premium is 2% of the life insurance benefit instead of saying the premium is $100,000.

My favorite way to get the conversation started on estate taxes is to show the client an estate tax chart. This chart lists various sizes of estates in one column. In the column next to these numbers is listed the estate taxes that would be owed. I ask the client to circle the number that is closest to the size of his estate. Then I point to the tax column and ask how his heirs would be able to get this tax bill paid within 9 months.

I do explain about the exemptions applicable in the process of arriving at the final calculation of the potential estate tax liability. Ask the clients again how would this amount of estate tax be paid in cash in 9 months. Let the clients think about it for a while. Then offer the perfect solution of using life insurance to pay the taxes.

Selling cash value life insurance for estate planning is a growing market. The need will always be there. More people each year are becoming multi-millionaires.

The wealthy tend to socialize with other wealthy people. Referrals in the estate planning market are very profitable. Good sources of referrals for estate planning cases are estate planning attorneys, CPAs, and luxury car sales people.

Buy Sell Life Insurance

One of the most important decisions in a business is the establishment of a funded buy sell agreement. A buy sell agreement is only a hopeful promise unless it is funded with life insurance. The life insurance lets the buyer and seller know that the funds will be there at death to make the promise a reality.

There are actually three contingencies that should be addressed in a properly designed buy sell agreement. A co-owner could die, become totally disabled or want to withdraw from the business. Most life insurance agents just sell term life insurance to cover death. They do not address the other two contingencies.

For disability, I recommend that you use disability buy sell insurance. There are a few companies that offer this coverage.

For a co-owner withdrawal, I recommend that the business build up a reserve of cash to provide a down payment for the payout of a withdrawing owner. This is followed by a series of continuing payments until the payout is completed.

The cash reserve that the company builds up should earn a decent rate of interest. It should be tax sheltered so that it does not add to the company's or owners' income taxes. It should be liquid and guaranteed.

These characteristics describe cash value life insurance. The company can get double duty from its life insurance policies. The buy sell life insurance covers the need in the event of the death of an owner and it builds cash values for the eventual withdrawal of one of the owners.

You should go to all your existing buy sell clients and talk them into covering all three contingencies with cash value life insurance and disability buy sell insurance.

Educate your clients and centers of influence about the three contingencies that need to be addressed in a properly designed buy sell agreement. In my experience, almost every buy sell agreement that I reviewed did not address the disability and withdrawal contingencies.

In fact, existing buy sell agreements need to be reviewed for accuracy. One agreement I reviewed had not been reviewed by the clients in 20 years and the values were grossly inaccurate. Another agreement had a typographical error. Instead of listing the buyout amount as $500,000 it had listed $50,000.

In both cases, the prospects had told me that their buy sell agreements were just fine and then I showed them the problems.

Your centers should introduce you to those businesses who have buy sell agreements as well as those who need to establish an agreement. Several times a year remind your clients and centers of this concept.

Key Person Benefit Plans

Business owners seek creative ways to attract, keep and reward key employees. Key persons appreciate bonuses. However, at a certain level of income, payroll taxes and income taxes reduce the value of cash bonuses.

Key Person Benefit Plans are also called Golden Handcuffs Plans and Executive Compensation Plans. These plans are ideal for providing ways to lock in key persons and keep them motivated.

The plans offer a retirement benefit as well as a pre-retirement death benefit. Cash value life insurance offers the funding that is needed for these plans. The cash values earn an attractive rate of return on a tax deferred basis. The plans are selective in who the participants are and the level of benefits for each.

With these plans, there may be increases in coverage required as incomes and benefits grow. Later, there may also be new participants to enroll and insure. I have found that once employers put a plan in place, they tend to add more participants periodically.

When enrolling a new participant, I ask the employer to let me describe the plan to the key employee. This gives me an opportunity to say good things about the employer. I get the employer to arrange a lunch meeting away from work. I like to say to the employee that "the employer is escrowing $1,000,000 (for example) for you payable to your heirs if you die before retirement at the rate of $100,000 a year for 10 years. If you live to retirement and have stayed with the employer, you will receive the $100,000 for 10 years." This really gets key employees excited.

The following describe several different plans: Defined Benefit Golden Handcuffs; Incentive Driven Golden Handcuffs; Growth Participation Plans; and, Leveraged Bonus Plans.

- Defined Benefit Golden Handcuffs is a program that provides a pre-defined retirement benefit for select key employees. The funding is a fixed premium each year. The employer can even choose a long vesting schedule (for example, 10 or 15 years).

- Incentive Driven Golden Handcuffs is the same as the Defined Benefit plan except that the funding is based upon a percentage of the employee's compensation as determined by the participant's performance at meeting his stated goals. The benefit is based on the cash values at the time of retirement.

- Growth Participation Plan is a plan that allows an employee, who is interested in having an ownership interest in the company, to participate in the growth of the company without the employer actually giving up ownership. This is utilized especially when the key person expresses a strong interest in ownership or is a candidate as a future purchaser of the business.

- Leveraged Bonus Plan is a plan that contributes the key employee's bonus to a cash value life insurance policy owned by the key employee but restricts access to the cash values for a pre-determined number of years or until the employer releases the restriction.

  How does the plan work? The employer purchases a cash value life insurance policy on the employee with the employer as owner and beneficiary. A legal agreement is signed defining the benefits for the employee. If the employee dies prematurely, the life insurance benefit will be enough to pay the promised benefit as a monthly income for a stated number of years.

  The employer will get a tax deduction for the proceeds paid to the employee or his heirs and earn interest on the proceeds received from the insurance company and that are waiting to be paid out.

At retirement, the employer will use the cash values to pay the monthly benefit over the stated number of years. The employer has the added leverage of the taxes saved from tax deducting these payments. The employer will also earn interest on the cash values not yet used. The combination of cash values, tax savings, and interest earnings are enough to pay the retirement benefit where the cash values alone may not be enough.

A sample presentation of the Golden Handcuffs Plan is in my first book, **The Prospect Says Yes! A Handbook for Selling Life Insurance.**

Charitable Planned Giving

In my second book, **A Life with Significance: Leaving a Legacy through Charitable Planned Giving**, I provided 21 examples of various ways to leave a legacy using charitable planned gifts. You can make a substantial amount of cash value life insurance sales in this market. Cash value life insurance is necessary to be able to provide coverage for life.

First, you will want to become well versed in charitable planned giving vehicles such as charitable remainder trusts, charitable lead trust, charitable annuities, foundations, etc. You can research these subjects on the internet, read some books or take a class.

Next, you will want to find out if there is an association of fundraising executives in your area. If yes, then join it. You will meet professionals in this field. They will help you learn more, may give you referrals and will enhance your reputation as a charitable planned giving expert.

Then, you need to let your clients, centers, friends and family know that you have become an expert in charitable planned giving.

Cash value life insurance can be the tool for giving. A donor can purchase a cash value life insurance policy naming a charity as the owner and beneficiary. That makes the premium tax deductible. In this way, a donor can leave a much larger gift to charity than the sum of the premiums. I have sold many of these policies.

Life insurance can be the vehicle that replaces a gift to charity. If a donor decides to give a gift of land, a building, highly appreciated stock, or some other asset to charity, the donor can purchase a life insurance policy for his heirs to replace the amount gifted to charity. The heirs will receive the proceeds of the life insurance in cash tax free. The taxes saved due to the charitable gift can fund the life insurance premiums for quite a few years.

In a charitable remainder trust, the donors are making an irrevocable gift to a charitable trust in exchange for a life income for the donors. After the donors die, all of the assets of the charitable trust go to the designated charities. The donors frequently use some of the income from the charitable remainder trust to buy cash value life insurance for their heirs to replace the gift to charity.

In my years of being a charitable planned giving expert, I sold more than $75 million of cash value life insurance in this market. The potential is huge.

Retirement Maximization

As clients look toward retirement, they can substantially improve their results with the addition of cash value life insurance.

Normally when a couple retires, they choose a retirement income payout option that is called "joint and 100% to the survivor" life income. This means that the income continues for life to two people until one of them dies. Then the income continues at the same level to the survivor. It ends when the survivor dies. Choosing this option also means choosing a lower income payout than if they had chosen a life income for one person only. The joint and survivor option is the safe option that most people take.

Alternatively, a couple could choose the higher income of a payout for one life only. The concern that the couple have is what happens to the survivor if the first one to die is the one who is receiving the income payout. The couple could buy a cash value life insurance policy on the life of the one who will receive the retirement income. If that person dies first, the survivor can live on the income provided by the life insurance proceeds. If the non-insured person dies first, then the insured person will continue to receive the higher retirement income payout and can decide if he wants to surrender the policy for its cash values.

Purchasing this policy early enough in life could result in getting the policy paid up by the time the couple retires. This is what I did. Run the numbers and you will see that doing retirement maximization is a very good option for many people planning for their retirement.

Asset Protection

In today's litigious society, many people are looking for ways to shelter their hard-earned assets from litigation or creditors. In most states, cash value life insurance is free from the claims of creditors and protected from litigation. Check your state's laws.

This could be important to medical and dental professionals as well as business owners and wealthy individuals. If you find someone concerned about being a target for litigation, let them know that you have a vehicle to shelter some of their assets. Let your clients and centers know that you have an asset protection vehicle for those who want it.

There is a limit on how much can be put into a life insurance policy (called the Modified Endowment Contract limit). Clients who are concerned about protecting their assets will buy large cash value life insurance policies and maximum fund them every year.

One agent that I know, told me that in this market he has sold numerous policies with annual premiums in the tens of thousands of dollars.

In Summary

Focusing on these situations with your more qualified prospects will lead to a substantial increase in your sales of cash value life insurance. The more you do of these types of sales, the more your reputation as an expert in these areas will grow. This will lead to more referrals and more sales. You will rise to a higher income.

4

Well Organized Activity

With your new focus on upgrading your prospects, you will want to get involved in activities that could put you in contact with qualified prospects. Consider the following:

- Join a service club – get involved and seek to become a leader in the club. Let others see that you are there to further the goals of the club as well as meet new friends.

- Join a country club – it will take time to get to know people without appearing to be prospecting. A lot of business does occur in country clubs but requires time and subtlety. Your spouse can be of real value in meeting people in the club. One on one lunches are effective.

- Activity clubs – this includes hiking, travel, tennis, etc. What is your interest? Follow it.

- Coaching – get involved in coaching your children's sports. If you do not have the skills, then be an assistant coach. There is always something that you can do. You will meet and get to know well the parents of the other children.

Consider your calendar. Is it full with productive activities? Like a doctor, you want your calendar full of actions that are the highest and best use of your time. You will want to ask yourself, is this the most thing I could be doing right now?

You will want to leave 10% of your work time unscheduled to be able to handle those items that are urgent but not necessarily important.

Each week you will want to schedule those activities that are part of your prospecting system. There are some good time management ideas in my first book, **The Prospect Says Yes! A Handbook for Selling Life Insurance.**

If you want to project a more professional image to your new qualified prospects, you will want to only schedule appointments during your scheduled work hours. You want to give the impression that your time is valuable and your family time is important to you.

You should have an experienced assistant. This person knows your business, knows your clients, confirms appointments, completes applications and gets them through underwriting, and monitors your prospecting system. A good assistant can make you a lot of money by freeing up your time. Pay your assistant very well so that you keep him and do not have to train a new one. If you do not have an experienced assistant, find one and hire him away.

Have a very professional looking office. You will want your initial appointment with your new qualified prospect to be in their office. Then all subsequent appointments should be in your office. If you ask, they will come.

A Final Note

If you apply the information in this book to your life insurance business, you should see a substantial increase in your income.

You will need to study and learn as much as you can in these areas.

I recommend that you get the CLU (Chartered Life Underwriter) designation and then perhaps get the ChFC (Chartered Financial Consultant) designation. The information you learn will be of great value in your sales. These credentials will enhance your reputation among other professionals and clients.

Be generous. I was impressed by a short book called **Rhinoceros Success** by Scott Alexander. He emphasized the importance of continuing to charge. Among other things he encourages us to be generous in our tipping and in our giving back to society.

This can be the fulfilling career that you want financially and in service to your clients.

Go for it!

VAN HOUTENISMS:
Words of Wisdom from Jim

✓ Never buy life insurance from a company that is younger than you.

✓ Never buy life insurance from a company that has a smaller net worth than you.

✓ Unseen and untold is unsold.

✓ See the People! STP.

✓ You talk differently to a client than a prospect.

✓ A widow is more conservative than a wife.

✓ Never buy a color TV from a guy on a street corner who is out of breath.

✓ The bitterness of poor quality lingers long after the sweetness of a cheap price.

✓ You should never allow your life insurance to die before you do.

✓ Selling is telling the truth in an attractive and convincing manner.

✓ Term life insurance is an expense, cash value life insurance is an asset.

✓ You cannot get to the promised land without going through the wilderness first.

✓ Eagles do not flock. You have to find them one at a time.

✓ When your purpose is to chop down the forest, you are not wasting time when you sharpen the axe.

✓ Elephants run in herds.

✓ China eggs never feathered anyone's nest.

✓ Sometimes you can make more money by saving taxes than by making more money.

About the Author

James A Van Houten, CLU, ChFC, MSFS, MSM

Jim Van Houten has over 50 years of experience providing financial services. He is the second generation of Van Houtens to work in the industry, providing financial services to clients from all over the nation.

Jim has 5 degrees and designations:

- Bachelor of Science in Finance (1969)
- Chartered Life Underwriter (CLU), advanced degree in life insurance (1971)
- Masters of Science in Financial Services (MSFS) (1979)
- Chartered Financial Consultant (ChFC), an advanced degree in financial consulting (1982)
- Masters of Science in Management (MSM) (1996)

Jim also owned one of the largest financial

services firm in Arizona and New Mexico from 1979 to 1997, and was a nationally recognized speaker.

His agency received 2 President's Trophy awards from MassMutual. The President's Trophy means that the agency was rated one of the top 5 in the nation.

Jim had over 35 years of qualification in the Million Dollar Round Table (MDRT), an international organization. He was a key speaker at the MDRT conference in 1980. Twice he qualified for the exclusive Top of the Table. Jim was Chair of the committee that determined the new qualifications for MDRT based on income rather than volume. This was a difficult task given the differences in monetary standards around the world. He was the founding Vice Chairman of the joint GAMC/MDRT Mentoring Council. He was a member of Arizona Business Leadership Association and served on its Board for 8 years.

In 2001 Jim co-founded with his son, Jameson, a financial planning and investment management firm. This firm is a Registered Investment Advisor (RIA) with over $300 million in assets under management.   Jim retired from the firm on August 2, 2013.

Jim's first book, "The Prospect Says Yes! A Handbook for Selling Life Insurance" was released in January, 2018. His second book, "A Life with Significance: Leaving a Legacy through Charitable Planned Giving" was released in January, 2020. His third book, "Buying Life Insurance: How to Make an Informed Choice" was released in October, 2020.

His community involvement has included: Charter Member of Paradise Valley United Methodist Church; member of the University of Arizona President's Club; past Board Member of Barrows Neurological Institute Foundation; past Board Member of the Arizona Friends of Foster Children

Foundation; retired Board Member of the Valley of the Sun YMCA after serving 37 years and its President in 1989; retired Board Member of the National Board of the YMCA of the USA serving for 8 years; past Board Member of the Claremont School of Theology; and, past Board Member of the Human Liberty ARTT Foundation. He is currently a member of the University of Arizona Cancer Center Advisory Board.

Jim has been happily married for over 52 years and has three adult sons, two daughters-in-law and five grandchildren. He lost a son in 2020. He served as a Little League coach for 18 years, on the Little League Board for 12 years, and a Boy Scout leader for 11 years. He enjoys reading, playing golf, biking and spending his summers in the cool weather of Show Low, AZ.

His website is www.jimvanhouten.com.

Made in the USA
Monee, IL
22 February 2021